Contents

FCE Cambridge First Certificate English Test-style exercises

T: GRADE 7 Trinity-style exercises (Grade 7)

This story is recorded in full.

These symbols indicate the beginning and end of the extracts linked to the listening activities.

Henry James (1913) by John Singer Sargent.

About the Author

Henry James was born in 1843 in New York City. His family was successful and cultured. They often travelled to Europe and lived there for long periods while Henry was growing up. Henry was educated by private tutors until he was twelve and was then sent to schools in Boulogne, Paris, Geneva, and Bonn. When his family returned to the United States, he finished his education at Newport, Rhode Island, and then entered Harvard Law School. However, a year later he left Harvard and started to think seriously about a career in writing.

He began writing reviews and critical essays which were published in *The Atlantic Monthly*, a prestigious American literary magazine. The magazine published his first novel – *Watch and Ward* – in 1871. Four years later, he spent a year in Paris in the company of prominent literary figures such as Turgenev, Flaubert, and Zola. He then went to London and published his second novel, *Roderick Hudson* (1875). After this, a number of novels, essays, and short stories followed. His best-known novels are: *The American* (1877), *The Europeans* (1878), *Daisy Miller* (1878), *Washington Square* (1881), *The Portrait of a Lady* (1881), *The Bostonians* (1886), *The Spoils of Poynton* (1897), *What Maisie Knew* (1897), *The Turn of the Screw* (1898), *The Awkward Age* (1899), *The Sacred Fount* (1901), *The Wings of the Dove* (1902), *The Ambassadors* (1903) and *The Golden Bowl* (1904).

A repeated theme in Henry James's fiction is the culture clash [1] between Americans and Europeans. As an American who spent most of his life in Europe, he was very well-placed to see the contrasts between these two cultures. His novels *Daisy Miller* and *The Portrait of a Lady* are based on this central idea. In both novels, the protagonist brings fresh American ideas to Europe. These are contrasted not only with the ideas of the Europeans, but also with those of Americans who have lived in Europe for a long time.

Daisy Miller was one of Henry James's most popular fictions. When it first appeared in 1878 it created great controversy: [2] some people liked Daisy's character, others did not. This controversy still exists in

1. **culture clash** : conflict between cultures, when people from different countries do not understand each other's customs.
2. **controversy** : a dispute or strong difference of opinion, especially public.

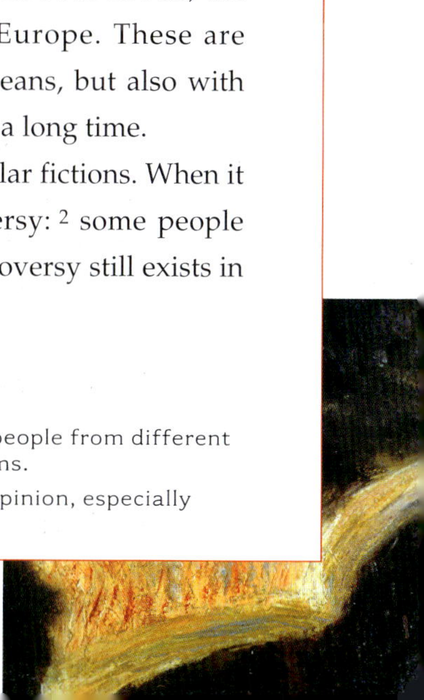

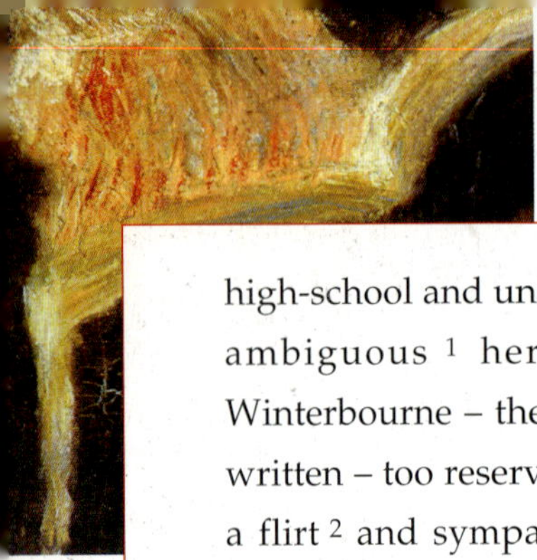

high-school and university classrooms today, as students discuss this ambiguous [1] heroine. Those who like Daisy usually find Winterbourne – the character from whose point of view the story is written – too reserved. Those who dislike Daisy usually consider her a flirt [2] and sympathise more with the character of Winterbourne. Both sides can find a lot of evidence in the text to support their opinions. The ambiguity is not just in the character of Daisy but also in the narrative itself: Henry James does not tell us what to think about his heroine; he leaves us to decide on our own.

In 1915 James became a British citizen. On New Year's Day 1916 he received the certificate of the Order of Merit – an order given to people for distinguished achievement.

He died on 28 February of the same year in Rye, south-east England.

1 Answer the following questions.

1 Where was Henry James born?
2 What was his family like?
3 Where did he go to school?
4 What famous writers did he meet in Europe?
5 What is one of the main themes of James's books?
6 What controversy does Daisy's character create?
7 What happened in James's life in 1915?

1. **ambiguous** : confusing, difficult to understand.
2. **flirt** : a sexually provocative person.

The Characters

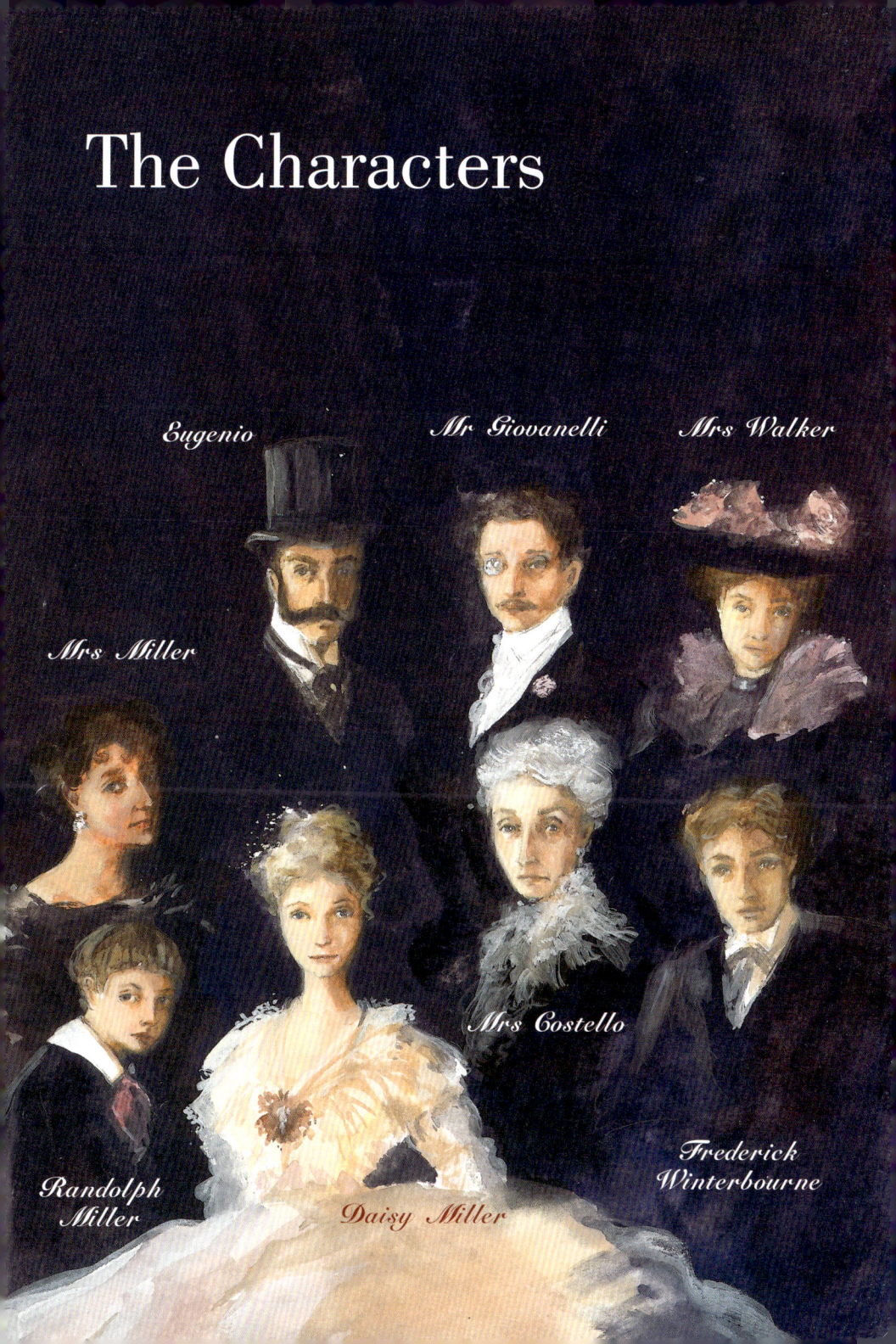

CHAPTER **ONE**

Vevey, Switzerland

Vevey is a beautiful little town on the shore [1] of a very blue lake in Switzerland. Tourism is the business of the place, and there are many hotels. American tourists particularly like the hotel called the Trois Couronnes. [2] Two years ago, a young American named Frederick Winterbourne spent a few days there. He had come from Geneva to see his aunt, Mrs Costello, who was staying at the Trois Couronnes. The morning after Winterbourne arrived in Vevey, his aunt had a headache, so he was free to sit in the garden of the hotel and enjoy its beauties. He sat by the wall, looking out at the Castle of Chillon, which stood on a small island in the lake.

Winterbourne was twenty-seven years old and had lived in Geneva for a long time. He had been at school and university

1. **shore** : the land beside the lake.
2. **the Trois Couronnes** : (French) the Three Crowns. This hotel still exists in Vevey.

there. When his friends spoke of him, they usually said that he was at Geneva 'studying'. When certain other people spoke of him they said that he spent so much time in Geneva because he was very attached to a lady who lived there — a European lady — a person older than himself. [1] None of his American friends had ever met this lady.

As Winterbourne was drinking his coffee in the garden of the Trois Couronnes, a small boy came up to him and said, 'Can you give me a lump of sugar?'

Winterbourne noticed that the boy spoke with an American accent. He pointed to the bowl of sugar and said, 'Take one, but I don't think sugar is good for little boys.'

The boy took three lumps of sugar. He put two in his pocket and one in his mouth. 'I eat sugar lumps,' he said, 'because I can't get any candy [2] here. American candy is the best.'

'And are American boys the best?' asked Winterbourne.

'I don't know,' said the child. 'I am an American boy. Are you an American man?'

'Yes.'

'American men are the best!' said the boy. Then, looking round, he added, 'Here comes my sister!'

Winterbourne looked up and saw a beautiful young lady coming towards them. 'American girls are the best!' he said cheerfully to his companion.

'My sister isn't the best,' said the boy. 'She's always criticising me.'

1. **a person older than himself** : this suggests that he is having a relationship with a married lady.
2. **candy** : (American English) sweets.

'That's probably your fault, not hers,' said Winterbourne. The young lady was dressed very elegantly in white. 'How pretty they are!' thought Winterbourne, preparing to get up.

The young lady stopped in front of him. She looked out over the blue lake. 'Randolph!' she said. 'What are you doing?'

'I'm talking to this man,' said Randolph. 'He's an American.'

Winterbourne stood up and said, 'Your brother and I have been discussing America.' He felt a little embarrassed: in Geneva, a gentleman could not speak to a young lady without being formally introduced. The young lady looked at him quickly then looked back at the lake.

'We've been talking about American candy,' said the boy. 'I don't want to go to Italy. I want to go home to America!'

'Are you going to Italy?' asked Winterbourne.

'Yes,' replied the young lady.

'Italy is a beautiful place.'

'But can you get any candy there?' asked Randolph.

'I think you've had enough candy,' said his sister, 'and Mother thinks so too.'

'Isn't this a splendid lake?' said Winterbourne. He no longer felt embarrassed, because he realised that the young lady did not feel embarrassed. When she looked at him, her eyes were honest and fresh. They were very pretty eyes. In fact, she was the prettiest girl he had seen for a long time. Her face was delicate but perhaps a little vulgar; [1] it was bright, sweet, and superficial. He thought that she might be a flirt, [2] but her

1. **vulgar** : (here) common, not of the style preferred by the upper classes of society.
2. **a flirt** : a sexually provocative, playful person.

expression was too innocent. Before long, she was speaking to him freely. She told him that she was going to Rome for the winter with her mother and Randolph. She told him that she was from New York State.

'Her name's Daisy Miller,' said Randolph. 'But that isn't her real name. Her real name is Annie P. Miller. And my father's name is Ezra B. Miller. He's back in New York State. He's got a big business. My father's rich.'

Miss Miller sat down and talked to Winterbourne while Randolph ran round the garden. She talked a lot — about her family, about her travels in Europe, about the hotels and the trains. Sometimes she looked at Winterbourne, and sometimes she looked out at the lake.

'The hotels are very good,' said Miss Daisy Miller. 'And I think Europe is perfectly sweet. I'm not disappointed — not at all. I knew a lot about Europe before I came here. I have lots of friends at home who have travelled in Europe, and they told me all about it. And back home I have lots of dresses from Paris...'

Winterbourne enjoyed this conversation. It was many years since he had heard a young girl talk so much.

'The only thing I don't like about Europe is the society,' [1] said Miss Miller. 'I like society. Last winter seventeen dinners were given in my honour, three of them by gentlemen.' She looked at him with her slightly monotonous smile and said, 'I've always had a lot of gentlemen friends.'

Winterbourne was amused, perplexed, and charmed. [2] He felt that he had lived too long in Geneva and therefore could no

1. **the society** : (here) the social life of the aristocracy/upper classes.
2. **Winterbourne was ... charmed** : he found her confusing, but entertaining and fascinating, too.

longer understand young American girls. He had never met a girl like this before. Was she simply a pretty girl from New York — were they all like that? Or was she an immoral young woman? She looked extremely innocent. Winterbourne decided that she

was just a pretty American flirt. He was happy to have found a formula to describe Miss Daisy Miller.

'Have you been to that old castle?' asked Miss Miller, pointing to the Castle of Chillon.

'Yes.'

'I want to go there, but Randolph doesn't want to go.'

'You could ask someone to stay with Randolph at the hotel.'

'Will you stay with him?'

'Can't I come to the Castle of Chillon with you?' asked Winterbourne. He was afraid that he had offended her, but she did not blush.[1] 'And your mother, of course,' he said very respectfully.

'Oh, Mother won't come,' said Miss Daisy Miller. 'She'll stay with Randolph, and Eugenio will stay too – he's our courier[2] – so we can go to the castle.'

Winterbourne thought, '"We" can only mean Miss Miller and I: it's too good to be true!'

At that moment Eugenio came up to them. He looked at Winterbourne with suspicion then said, 'Lunch is ready, mademoiselle.'

'Oh, Eugenio!' Daisy Miller replied, 'I'm going to that old castle anyway.'

'Really?' said Eugenio. He looked at Winterbourne disrespectfully.

Miss Miller blushed a little. 'We are going, aren't we?' she asked Winterbourne.

'I won't be happy until we go!' he said.

'And you are staying at this hotel?' she continued. 'And you really are an American?'

'I'll introduce you to my aunt, Mrs Costello. She can tell you all about me.'

'Oh, well,' said Daisy Miller, 'we'll go some day.' She smiled at Winterbourne and walked back to the hotel with Eugenio.

1. **blush** : go red in the face from embarrassment.
2. **courier** : (here) a servant who makes travel arrangements and translates.

Go back to the text

FCE 1 Comprehension

For questions 1-6, choose the correct answer (A, B, C or D) which you think fits best according to the text.

1 Frederick's friends said that he spent a lot of time in Geneva because

A ☐ he was a good friend of an older woman.
B ☐ he was studying.
C ☐ he enjoyed spending time with his aunt, who lived there.
D ☐ he did not want to return to America.

2 Frederick says that American girls are the best because

A ☐ he wants to make fun of Randolph.
B ☐ he wants to make a joke.
C ☐ he prefers women of his own country.
D ☐ he sees Daisy and thinks she is very attractive.

3 Frederick stopped feeling embarrassed in Daisy's company because

A ☐ she was so pretty.
B ☐ Randolph introduced her to him.
C ☐ she was not embarrassed talking with him.
D ☐ he felt that she was a flirt.

4 Daisy is a bit disappointed with Europe because

A ☐ she has not been to many dinners.
B ☐ she does not like the trains.
C ☐ she does not like the hotels.
D ☐ she does not like European gentlemen.

5 Frederick feels that he cannot judge Daisy correctly because

A ☐ he has lived in Geneva for too long.
B ☐ she does not blush when she talks to him.
C ☐ he has not known her long enough.
D ☐ she is different from other American girls that he has known.

6 Daisy says that she and Frederick will go to the castle alone because

A ☐ her mother and Eugenio must stay with her brother.

B ☐ her mother is not interested in old castles.

C ☐ she wants to be alone with Frederick.

D ☐ Eugenio is suspicious of Frederick.

2 The correct formula

Answer the following questions.

1 Frederick thinks of three possible 'categories' that describe Daisy. What are they?

A ....

B ....

C ....

2 Which one does he finally decide is right for her? Why did he initially reject this formula?

3 Why do you think he is so interested in finding the correct formula to describe Daisy Miller?

FCE 3 *Daisy Miller*: Henry's answer to William

For questions 1-10, read this text about Henry James's fear of losing contact with America, and decide which answer A, B, C or D best fits the space.

Frederick Winterbourne thinks that
he can no **(1)** .... understand other Americans.
This certainly reflects a worry of Henry James himself.
Although he was **(2)** .... in New York, James went to school
(3) .... Geneva, and as a young man he gradually decided
(4) .... set his fiction in Europe, and not America.
His older brother, the philosopher and psychologist William James,
(5) .... Henry he must be careful:
he could become too European in his writing
and he **(6)** .... lose contact with other Americans.
Daisy Miller, in part, seems to be Henry's response

to his brother's criticisms. He (7) .... the character of Frederick, who (8) .... difficulty understanding a young American woman because he has lived in Geneva for (9) .... long.
Henry James clearly understood both the confused Frederick and the American Daisy (10) .... well.

1	A anymore	B yet	C longer	D already
2	A born	B lived	C from	D home
3	A to	B in	C at	D by
4	A the	B on	C because	D to
5	A said	B told	C ordered	D made
6	A could	B may	C can	D must
7	A made	B built	C created	D did
8	A does	B gets	C takes	D has
9	A very	B much	C greatly	D too
10	A much	B many	C greatly	D very

Before you read

1 Look at the words in the box below and choose the correct one in order to complete the text (you will not need to use four of the words). Then listen to the beginning of Chapter Two to check your answers.

paid little so noticed in to next at very better

The (1) .... day, Winterbourne went to see his aunt in her room.
'I hope you're feeling (2) ....,' he said.
'A (3) ....,' replied Mrs Costello. She was a rich widow and an important figure of New York society. She had a long pale face and a lot of white hair. She had two married sons (4) .... New York and a third son who was travelling in Europe but had not come to see her. Winterbourne had come (5) .... Vevey just to see his aunt. She often told him that he (6) .... more attention to her than her own sons did.

CHAPTER **TWO**

Mrs Costello

The next day, Winterbourne went to see his aunt in her room. 3

'I hope you're feeling better,' he said.

'A little,' replied Mrs Costello. She was a rich widow [1] and an important figure of New York society. She had a long pale face and a lot of white hair. She had two married sons in New York and a third son who was travelling in Europe but had not come to see her. Winterbourne had come to Vevey just to see his aunt. She often told him that he paid more attention to her than her own sons did. END

'Have you noticed an American family here at the hotel?' asked Winterbourne. 'A family called Miller?'

'A mother, a daughter, a little boy, and a courier? Oh, yes! I've noticed them!' said Mrs Costello. 'I confess I'm very exclusive, but in New York you have to be. There are so many vulgar people in society these days. That Miller family is a perfect example.'

1. **widow** : a woman whose husband is dead.

'The young girl is very pretty,' said Winterbourne.

'Of course she's pretty, but she's very vulgar. She's too friendly with the courier. Her mother is just as bad. They treat the courier like a family friend. He probably eats dinner with them. I'm sure they've never seen a man with such good manners, such fine clothes, so like a gentleman! He sits with them in the garden and smokes cigars.'

'I see what you mean, of course,' said the young man, 'but I met the young lady in the garden. I'd like to introduce her to you.'

'I'm afraid I can't meet her! Why do you want to introduce her to me?'

'To guarantee my respectability.'

'But who'll guarantee hers?'

'Ah, you're cruel!' said the young man. 'She's a very nice girl and completely unsophisticated. I'm going to take her to the Castle of Chillon.'

'Really? And how long had you known her when this plan was formed?' asked Mrs Costello in surprise.

'Half an hour!' said Winterbourne, smiling.

'Oh, what a terrible girl!' cried Mrs Costello. 'My dear Frederick, you've been away from America too long. You're too innocent. You'll make some great mistake.'

'I'm not so innocent!'

'You're too guilty, then!'

Winterbourne sat in silence for a while then said, 'So I can't introduce her to you?'

'No. I can't accept a girl who talks to strangers [1] in hotels.'

1. **strangers** : (here) people who she has not been formally introduced to.

'But don't all the young girls in America do that sort of thing?'

'My grand-daughters don't do that sort of thing!' said Mrs Costello.

Winterbourne had heard his pretty cousins in New York described as 'terrible flirts'. If Miss Daisy Miller did things that his cousins did not do, she must be very unconventional [1] indeed. Winterbourne was impatient to see her again.

That evening, he met Miss Daisy Miller walking in the garden. She seemed very pleased to see him.

'Have you been walking here all alone?' he asked.

'No,' she replied. 'I've been walking with Mother, but she's gone to find Randolph. She wants him to go to bed. He doesn't like to go to bed before eleven.'

Winterbourne and Daisy walked in the garden together. 'I hear that your aunt is very exclusive,' said Daisy. 'I want to meet her. I know I'll like her.'

Winterbourne was embarrassed. 'I'm afraid she often has headaches,' he said.

Daisy looked at him for a moment then said, 'She doesn't want to meet me! Why don't you just say so? You needn't be afraid. I'm not afraid!' She gave a little nervous laugh.

Winterbourne wanted to comfort her. He wanted to tell her that his aunt was a snob [2] and that her opinion was not important. But just then a lady came into the garden and stood at a distance from them, looking out at the lake.

'Oh. There's Mother,' said Daisy Miller.

1. **unconventional** : not conforming to the normal rules of society.
2. **a snob** : someone who is not interested in anything he/she considers socially inferior.

Mrs Miller was a small nervous-looking person, very elegantly dressed, with enormous diamonds in her ears.

'I should go,' said Winterbourne.

'No, no,' replied Daisy. 'I want to introduce you to Mother. I always introduce my gentlemen friends to Mother.'

'She doesn't seem to want to be introduced to me,' said Winterbourne, since Mrs Miller still had not looked at him.

'She's very shy,' Daisy explained, then she took Winterbourne over to meet her mother. 'Mother, this is Mr Winterbourne,' said Daisy very prettily. Yes, Miss Daisy Miller was vulgar, as Mrs Costello had said, but Winterbourne thought she also had an unusual and delicate grace.

'Did you convince Randolph to go to bed?' asked Daisy.

'No,' replied Mrs Miller. 'He won't go.'

'He won't do what he's told,' said Daisy. 'He won't go to that castle either, so I'm going with Mr Winterbourne.'

'It's a beautiful castle, Mrs Miller,' said Winterbourne. 'Don't you want to see it?'

'No, thank you,' said Mrs Miller. 'Daisy will go, though.'

Winterbourne thought how very different Mrs Miller was from the vigilant mothers of Geneva. They never let their daughters go anywhere unprotected.

'Mr Winterbourne,' said Daisy suddenly. 'Will you take me out in a boat?'

'Now?'

'Yes, now.'

'Well, Annie Miller!' cried her mother.

'I'm sure that Mr Winterbourne wants to take me out in a boat!' said Daisy, laughing.

'But what time is it? I'm sure it's time to go to bed!' said Mrs Miller.

'It's eleven o'clock, madam,' said a voice from the darkness.

'Oh, Eugenio,' said Daisy. 'I'm going out in a boat!'

'At eleven o'clock, mademoiselle?'

'Please tell her she can't go,' said Mrs Miller to the courier.

'Does mademoiselle want to go alone?' asked Eugenio.

'No,' Mrs Miller replied. 'She wants to go with this gentleman!'

Eugenio looked at Winterbourne, then he said, 'As mademoiselle pleases.'

'Why don't you say no?' said Daisy to the courier. 'I don't want to go now.' She turned to Winterbourne, smiled, and said, 'Good night. I hope you're disgusted or disappointed or something.'

'I'm confused,' said Winterbourne. He stood and watched the two ladies and their courier as they walked back into the hotel.

Go back to the text

1 Comprehension

Say whether the following statements are true (T) or false (F). Then correct the false ones.

		T	F
1	Mrs Costello's husband lived in New York.	☐	☐
2	Mrs Costello thought that Eugenio was a fine gentleman.	☐	☐
3	Mrs Costello refused to meet Daisy because she was American.	☐	☐
4	Frederick's pretty cousins did not talk to strangers.	☐	☐
5	Frederick did not want to introduce his aunt to Daisy.	☐	☐
6	Daisy understood the real reason why Mrs Costello did not want to meet her.	☐	☐
7	Mrs Miller did not want Daisy to go out in a boat with Frederick because he was a stranger.	☐	☐
8	Daisy wanted Eugenio to tell her not to go to the castle in a boat.	☐	☐
9	Frederick did not understand whether Daisy wanted to go to the castle with him or not.	☐	☐

2 Introductions

Answer the following questions.

1 Why does Frederick want to introduce Daisy to his aunt?
   - A Because he wants them to become friends as they both come from New York.
   - B Because he wants to show Daisy that he comes from high-class society.
   - C Because he wants to show his aunt that Daisy is beautiful and sophisticated.

2 Does Mrs Costello agree to the introduction? Why is this is?

3 What adjectives does Frederick use to describe Daisy in this chapter?

4 What adjectives does Mrs Costello use to describe Daisy?

T: GRADE 7

3 Topic – Youth Culture

In formal European society in the late 1800s, young men and women were never alone together. They always met when they were with other adults. Compare this with the situation today. Use the following questions to help you.

- Where do young men and women meet today?
- Where did young men and women of your parents' generation use to meet? What about your grandparents' generation?
- Daisy's behaviour with Frederick seemed 'vulgar' to Mrs Costello. Would it be strange in your country today?

4 Wordsearch – opposites attract

Complete the opposites of the words below (1-11) and then find them in the wordsearch. All the words are from this chapter.

1 refined : v_ _ _ _ _

2 ugly : _ _ _ _ _ y

3 enemy : _ r _ _ _ _

4 kind : c _ _ _ _

5 light : d _ _ _ _ _ _ _

6 outgoing : _ h _

7 wonderful : _ _ _ _ _ _ l _

8 innocent : _ u _ _ _ _

9 rarely : _ f _ _ _

10 small : e _ _ _ _ _ _ _

11 relaxed : _ _ _ v _ _ _

G	P	R	E	T	T	Y	R	B	C	V	G
E	T	F	V	R	U	Y	A	K	R	I	E
L	G	R	D	U	B	J	E	A	U	G	M
O	U	I	O	G	L	Z	Z	I	E	I	E
F	I	E	A	P	W	G	H	D	L	L	T
T	L	N	S	H	Y	Y	A	A	K	A	E
E	T	D	N	P	L	T	U	R	F	N	R
N	Y	L	O	D	L	Y	I	K	X	T	R
C	J	G	G	K	T	U	Q	N	S	U	I
Z	W	U	O	S	B	N	D	E	O	D	B
O	E	N	O	R	M	O	U	S	K	G	L
C	N	E	R	V	O	U	S	S	M	P	E

Before you read

4 FCE

1 Listening

Listen to the beginning of Chapter Three and choose the best answer A, B or C.

1 Frederick and Daisy went to the castle
- A ☐ two days later.
- B ☐ three days later.
- C ☐ two weeks later.

2 Where did Daisy and Frederick meet for their trip to the castle?
- A ☐ in the restaurant
- B ☐ by the main door of the hotel
- C ☐ in front of Daisy's room

3 How did Daisy seem to feel about the trip?
- A ☐ excited
- B ☐ happy
- C ☐ disappointed

4 Who decided to go to the castle by boat?
- A ☐ Daisy
- B ☐ Frederick
- C ☐ Mrs Miller

5 How did Frederick feel when he was with Daisy on the boat?
- A ☐ bored
- B ☐ embarrassed
- C ☐ proud

CHAPTER **THREE**

The Castle of Chillon

4

Two days later, Winterbourne and Miss Miller went to the Castle of Chillon. They met by the main door of the hotel. Daisy ran down the stairs, with a bright smile on her face. She was simply but elegantly dressed. All the couriers, servants, and foreign tourists in the main hall stared [1] at her. To Winterbourne their trip to the castle seemed romantic: he thought of it as an adventure, and he hoped that she did too, but in this respect he was disappointed. She seemed happy but not excited. She did not blush when she looked at him or when she saw that other people were looking at her. Winterbourne wanted to go to the castle in a carriage, [2] over the wooden bridge that connected the island to

1. **stared** : looked at for a long time.
2. **carriage** : a vehicle pulled by horses.

the shore, but Daisy said that she preferred to go in the little steamboat.[1] She liked the breeze[2] on the lake.

The steamboat was very crowded, and the people stared at Miss Daisy Miller. Winterbourne thought, 'Will she embarrass me by

1. **steamboat** : a boat operated by a steam engine.
2. **breeze** : a light, gentle wind.

talking too loudly or laughing too much?' But soon he forgot those anxieties. He stood smiling at her and listening to her conversation. He had agreed with his aunt when she had said that Miss Daisy Miller was vulgar, but now he felt uncertain. 'Is she really vulgar?' he asked himself, watching her pretty face. Winterbourne did not feel embarrassed by her at all. In fact, he felt rather proud to be with such a beautiful and elegant young lady.

She talked a lot, and most of her conversation was about the things she had seen and done. She asked him many questions about his life and opinions, and she told him about herself and her family. At one point, she turned to him and said, 'Why are you so serious?'

'Serious?' asked the young man in surprise. 'I thought I was grinning from ear to ear!' [1]

'You look as if you were taking me to a funeral. If that's a grin, your ears are very close together!'

'I'm having the time of my life,' [2] said Winterbourne quietly.

She looked at him for a moment then laughed: 'I like to make you say those things! You're a strange mixture!'

It was a beautiful sunny day. At the castle, they walked around alone except for the guide. Winterbourne asked the guide not to hurry, to let them pause wherever they pleased. He gave the guide a generous tip [3] as he said this. The guide thought he was being paid to leave them in peace, and he did so.

Daisy ran up the stairs and looked out of the little windows with great enthusiasm, but Winterbourne could see that she was not really interested in the old castle. She asked him about the history of the place, and when he had explained it, she said, 'You certainly know a lot. Do you want to come travelling with us and teach Randolph?'

'I'm afraid I can't,' Winterbourne replied.

'Why not? You don't work. You're not in business. Why can't you do what you want?'

1. **grinning from ear to ear** : smiling very widely.
2. **I'm having the time of my life** : this is the best experience I've ever had.
3. **tip** : the extra money paid for good service.

'There are things I must do in Geneva. In fact, I must go back there tomorrow.'

'I don't believe it!' cried Miss Daisy Miller.

'I'm afraid it's true.'

'Well, Mr Winterbourne, I think you're horrible!' For the next ten minutes she kept repeating that he was horrible. Poor Winterbourne was confused. No young lady had ever done him the honour of being so agitated by his departure.

'I suppose you must be going to see a lady there!' said Daisy.

'No, I'm not!' protested Winterbourne, but he thought, 'How does she know about the lady?' He was surprised by her insight [1] and by the honest way she confronted him about the lady in Geneva. Miss Daisy Miller seemed to him an extraordinary mixture of innocence and vulgarity.

'Does she never allow you out for more than three days?' asked Daisy sarcastically. 'Doesn't she give you a vacation in the summer? But never mind. I'll forgive you if you promise to come to Rome in the winter.'

'Certainly I'll come,' said Winterbourne. 'My aunt has a house in Rome, and I've promised to visit her there this winter.'

'I don't want you to come for your aunt,' said Miss Daisy Miller. 'I want you to come for me.'

After this, Daisy lost all interest in the castle and the lake. Winterbourne found a carriage to take them back to the hotel. On the journey back, she was very quiet.

1. **insight** : ability to understand things that are not obvious.

Go back to the text

1 Comprehension

Answer the following questions.

1 How was Daisy dressed for the trip to the castle?
2 How did Frederick know that Daisy did not see their trip as a romantic adventure?
3 How did Daisy act on the boat?
4 Why was Frederick proud to be with her?
5 How did Daisy make fun of Frederick when they were on the boat?
6 What was the real reason for Daisy's questions about the history of the castle?
7 Why did Daisy think that Frederick had to go back to Geneva to see a lady?

FCE 2 Write about it

Imagine you are Frederick's friend. Frederick wrote you a letter about Daisy. He told you that he was very confused about her.
Write him a letter of 120-180 words and tell him what *you* think about Daisy. Consider the following:

- Is Daisy a flirt?
- Is she in love with Frederick?
- Do you think your friend is in love with Daisy?

You can begin your letter like this:

Dear Frederick,
Your letter was very interesting! ....
....
....
....
I hope this helps you.
Your friend,
William

FCE **3** **For questions 1-4, complete the second sentence so that it has a similar meaning to the first sentence, using the word given. Do not change the word given. You must use between two and five words, including the word given. There is an example at the beginning (0).**

0 Winterbourne sat in silence for a while
talking
Winterbourne ...stopped talking... for a while.

1 Winterbourne was impatient to see her again.
not
Winterbourne .... to see her again.

2 You needn't be afraid.
have to
You .... afraid.

3 She was simply but elegantly dressed.
simple
She .... clothes.

4 The steamboat was very crowded.
were
There .... on the steamboat.

4 Summing it up

Number the paragraphs in the correct order to make a summary of the first three chapters.

A ☐ Daisy guessed the reason for his refusal: he had a lady friend in Geneva. She became angry.

B ☐ Soon after they arrived at the castle, Daisy asked Frederick if he wanted to travel with her and her family. He said that he couldn't.

C ☐ Even though Frederick was a stranger, she did not hesitate to talk to him. She even accepted his invitation to visit the Castle of Chillon.

D ☐ Later Frederick asked his aunt about Daisy. She told him that Daisy and her family were extremely vulgar and she did not want to meet them.

E ☐ But she told him that she would forgive him if he came to visit her in Rome that winter. Frederick agreed.

F ☐ There he met a little American boy and his older sister, Daisy. She was very different from all the other girls Frederick had met.

G ☐ Despite his aunt's opinion, Frederick and Daisy took the steamboat to the castle. Frederick was proud to be seen with such a pretty young lady.

H ☐ A young American called Frederick came to the town of Vevey, Switzerland to visit his aunt. One morning he was sitting alone in the garden of the hotel.

5 Speaking

The Castle of Chillon is a popular tourist attraction in Switzerland – it receives over 300,000 visitors every year.

1 What are the most famous tourist attractions in your country? Have you visited them?

2 Why do you think they are so popular?

3 Find some pictures of a particular tourist attraction in your country. Working in groups, try to persuade the rest of your classmates to go and visit it. Talk about what there is to see and do, and explain why you think they will like it.

Before you read

5 FCE

1 Listen to the beginning of Chapter Four and complete the sentences.

1 Winterbourne went to Rome in ....

2 Daisy Miller's gentleman-friend has very elegant ....

3 Mrs Costello thinks the Miller family are .... people.

4 Winterbourne thinks they are just .... and ....

5 Mrs Costello thinks that being bad is the same as being ....

CHAPTER **FOUR**

Meeting in Rome

1 The next day, Winterbourne returned to Geneva, but in January he went to Rome, as promised. On his first evening there, his aunt said to him, 'That Miller family is here. The girl goes out alone with Italian men — well-known Roman fortune-hunters. [1] And she takes them to respectable people's houses! It's a great scandal. [2] When she comes to a party, she brings with her a gentleman with elegant manners and a splendid moustache.' [3] 5

'And where's her mother?' asked Winterbourne.

'I've no idea,' Mrs Costello replied. 'They're terrible people.'

Winterbourne thought for a moment. 'They're just very ignorant and innocent. I really don't believe that they're bad people.'

1. **fortune-hunters** : people who try to marry someone with a lot of money.
2. **scandal** : shocking and immoral situation.
3. **moustache** : hair on a man's upper lip.

'They're very vulgar,' said his aunt. 'You may say that being vulgar is different from being bad, but I don't see the difference.'

2 Winterbourne had imagined Miss Daisy Miller looking out of her window in a Roman hotel rather sadly, waiting for him to arrive. This new picture of her surrounded by Roman fortune-hunters did not please him, so he did not go to visit her on his first day in Rome. Instead he went to the house of Mrs Walker, an American

lady he knew from Geneva, where her children were at school. She lived in the Via Gregoriana. Winterbourne found her in a little red drawing-room [1] full of afternoon sunshine. As he was talking to Mrs Walker, the servant came in and announced, 'Mrs Miller!'. Then Randolph entered the room, followed by Daisy and her mother.

1. **drawing-room** : a room where people sit, relax, and talk.

'Well!' said Daisy in surprise. 'I didn't know you were in Rome! Why didn't you come to see me?'

'I only arrived yesterday,' replied Winterbourne.

3 Randolph looked around the room and said, 'We've got a bigger place than this. The walls are all gold.'

'Oh, Randolph!' said Mrs Miller nervously.

'Are you enjoying Rome?' Winterbourne asked her.

'Well, I'm rather disappointed,' she replied. 'We'd heard so much about it, but we've seen other places I like much better.'

'Really? Which places?'

'For example, Zurich,' said Mrs Miller. 'I think Zurich is lovely, and we hadn't heard much about it.'

'The best place we've been is the *City of Richmond*,' said Randolph.

'He means the ship that brought us to Europe,' Mrs Miller explained. 'Randolph enjoyed the *City of Richmond*.'

'It's the best place I've seen,' said Randolph, 'but it was going the wrong way.'[1]

4 'I hope Miss Miller is enjoying Rome,' said Winterbourne.

'Oh, yes,' replied Mrs Miller. 'Daisy loves Rome. The society is splendid. She's invited to many people's houses. She goes out much more frequently than I do. And she knows a lot of gentlemen here. Yes, she loves Rome. Of course, young ladies are always happier in a place if they know a lot of gentlemen there.'

5 Daisy had been talking to Mrs Walker, but now she turned to Winterbourne and said, 'I've been telling Mrs Walker how horrible you were to me in Vevey.'

1. **it was going the wrong way** : Randolph means it was going to Europe, but he wanted it to return to America.

Winterbourne was rather irritated. She did not seem to appreciate the fact that he had travelled from Geneva without stopping at Bologna or Florence, simply because he was impatient to see her. He remembered an American friend of his who had told him that American women — the pretty ones — were the most demanding and least grateful [1] women in the world.

'My dear young lady!' cried Winterbourne. 'Have I come all the way to Rome just to hear you criticise me?'

6 But Daisy ignored him. She turned back to Mrs Walker and said, 'Thank you for inviting us to your party. We gladly accept the invitation.'

'I'm delighted to hear it,' replied Mrs Walker.

'I've got a lovely dress.'

'I'm very sure of that.'

'But I want to ask you a favour: can I please bring a friend?'

'Certainly,' said Mrs Walker, smiling at Mrs Miller. 'Any friend of yours is welcome.'

'Oh, they're not *my* friends,' said Mrs Miller with a nervous smile. 'I've never met them!'

'He's a very close friend of mine,' said Daisy. 'Mr Giovanelli.'

Mrs Walker was silent for a moment. She looked quickly at Winterbourne then said, 'Mr Giovanelli is welcome to come to the party.'

'He's an Italian,' continued Daisy serenely. 'He's the most handsome [2] man in the world, except for Mr Winterbourne. He

1. **grateful** : thankful, showing appreciation.
2. **handsome** : beautiful, attractive (used for men).

knows lots of Italians, but he wants to meet some Americans. He's very clever and perfectly lovely!'

7 'Daisy,' said Mrs Miller. 'It's time to go back to the hotel.'

'You go,' Daisy replied with a smile. 'I'm going to the Pincio [1] for a walk.'

'She's going to walk with Mr Giovanelli,' said Randolph.

'Alone, my dear?' asked Mrs Walker. 'And at this hour? I don't think it's safe.'

'Neither do I,' said Mrs Miller. 'You'll get the fever!' [2]

'I'm not going alone,' said Daisy to Mrs Walker. 'I'm going with the beautiful Mr Giovanelli.'

'My dear young friend,' said Mrs Walker. 'Don't go to the Pincio at this hour to meet a beautiful Italian.'

'Oh!' said Daisy. 'I don't want to do anything improper. [3] Perhaps Mr Winterbourne will walk to the Pincio with me. That'll solve the problem.'

Winterbourne agreed, and they walked together down the stairs and past Mrs Miller's carriage, in which Eugenio was waiting.

'Goodbye, Eugenio,' cried Daisy. 'I'm going for a walk.'

1. **the Pincio** : historical gardens in Rome. The Pincio was built at the beginning of the 19th century and became a popular place for people to meet and observe others. (See page 59 for Henry James's impressions of the Pincio.)
2. **the fever** : (here) malaria, known as 'Roman fever' at the time.
3. **improper** : not respectable or socially appropriate.

Go back to the text

1 Comprehension

Say whether the following statements are true (T) or false (F), and then correct the false ones.

		T	F
1	People were shocked that Daisy went out alone with men.	☐	☐
2	Frederick hoped that Daisy had missed him.	☐	☐
3	Frederick did not visit Daisy as soon as he arrived in Rome because he did not know where she lived.	☐	☐
4	Randolph was happiest in Zurich.	☐	☐
5	Frederick did not stop in Bologna or Florence because he preferred Rome.	☐	☐
6	Daisy criticised Frederick for not coming to Rome until January.	☐	☐
7	Mrs Miller thought it was improper for Daisy to be alone with Mr. Giovanelli at the Pincio.	☐	☐
8	Frederick decided to accompany Daisy to see Mr Giovanelli.	☐	☐

FCE 2

Chapter Four has been divided into seven parts. Choose from the list (A-H) the title which best summarises each part (1-7). There is one extra title which you do not need to use. The first one has been done for you.

A ☐ Happier at Sea
B ☐ Unappreciative
C ☐ A Long Journey to Happiness
D [1] The Wrong People in the Right Places
E ☐ One More Guest
F ☐ Girls Just Want to Have Fun
G ☐ Health and Reputation in Danger
H ☐ A Disappointing Reality

3 Crossword

Complete the crossword using the clues given below. All the answers are words taken from Chapters 1-4.

Across

4 Articles of women's clothing.

5 Extra money you pay for good service.

7 Uninteresting because it doesn't vary.

8 The past participle of 'see'.

9 Made two people know each other (for the first time).

11 A delicate wind.

13 Sad (because the reality is not as you hoped).

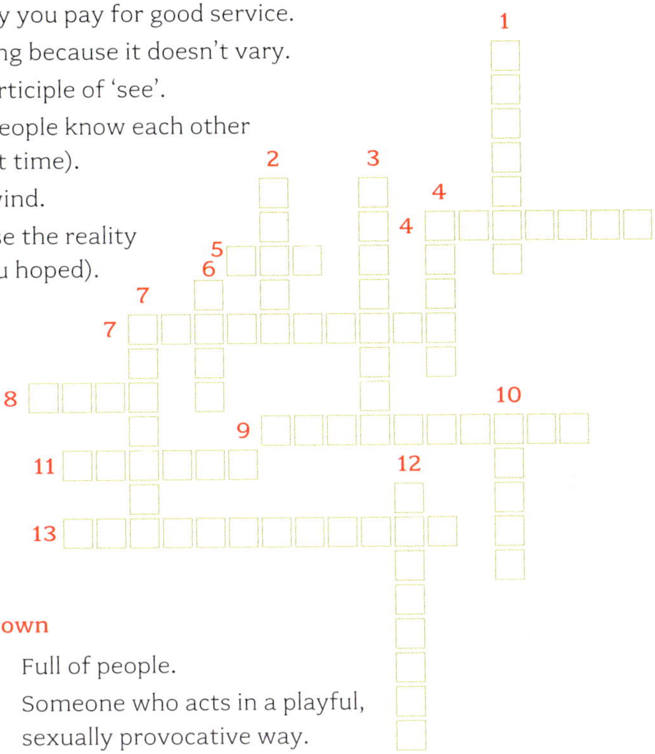

Down

1 Full of people.

2 Someone who acts in a playful, sexually provocative way.

3 Not socially acceptable.

4 A flower; a girl's name in this book.

6 Someone who feels socially superior to others.

7 Ways of acting and behaving.

10 The American word for sweets.

12 If your head hurts you have a ________.

Young Women
in the Nineteenth Century

In nineteenth-century Italy, young unmarried ladies were protected by their families so that there could be no possibility of scandal. A young lady was never allowed to walk alone or in the company of gentlemen. Young Italian ladies used to spend most of their time at home with frequent visits to church in the company of older women. The only way a young lady could meet men was when her parents invited them to the house or when she went, with her parents, to the homes of her parents' friends. Most marriages were therefore the product of careful selection by the young lady's family. This rigid control of women's lives has a long history in Italy and in Europe in general. In fact, it could be argued that the rigid control of women's lives is just one of the many consequences of having a long history: old countries tend to be more conventional than young ones.

In 1878 – the year in which Daisy Miller was written – the United States of America was a very young country indeed: independence from Britain had been won just over a century before. Young ladies in the United States had a little more liberty and there was already a lively feminist movement, as there was in Britain. Italy had no such movement until the twentieth century, although during the Renaissance well-known writers such as Ariosto expressed surprisingly advanced ideas about women's roles and capacities.

So why was there greater freedom for women in the United States than in Italy in the nineteenth century? It is an interesting question, but one that is difficult to answer. Here are three possible reasons:

1. the United States was a very young country at the time which made change more possible;

The Wyndham Sisters (1899), detail, by John Singer Sargent.

2. the Americans were still strongly influenced by English writers and thinkers. This probably contributed to the development of the American feminist movement because a strong women's movement had been growing in Britain for many decades before the 1870s. The issue was, by that time, a central topic of debate in English newspapers, magazines, and novels;
3. the feminist movement in the United States had grown up with the movement for the abolition [1] of slavery.

1. **abolition** : the end of.

This last reason needs further explanation. The American Civil War (1861-5) had resulted in the liberation of the slaves. The political movement that had supported the freeing of the slaves was known as the Abolition Movement. During the 1840s and 1850s, Abolition was a central issue of debate in American literature and life. At the same time, American feminists (who were often also members of the Abolitionist movement) began writing books and newspaper articles pointing out [1] the similarities between the position of slaves and the position of women.

One of these American feminists, Margaret Fuller, came to Italy in 1846, married an Italian, and became involved in the fight for a united Italian Republican government in Italy. This example demonstrates that there were at least some American women in the nineteenth century who had the freedom to do far more unconventional things than poor Daisy Miller ever does.

1 Say whether the following statements are true (T) or false (F), and then correct the false ones.

		T	F
1	Young unmarried women in nineteenth-century Italy often went out alone.	☐	☐
2	Marriages in nineteenth-century Italy were based on love.	☐	☐
3	American women had more freedom than Italian women in the late 1800s.	☐	☐
4	The feminist movement began in the United States during the 1740s.	☐	☐
5	American feminists compared the position of women to that of the slaves.	☐	☐
6	Margaret Fuller, an American feminist, fought against a united Italian Republican government.	☐	☐

1. **pointing out** : directing attention towards, indicating.

CHAPTER **FIVE**

Introducing Mr Giovanelli

As they walked, Daisy told Winterbourne all about her experiences in Rome. 'We have very beautiful rooms at the hotel,' she said. 'We'll stay here all winter, unless we die of the fever, and in that case we'll stay even longer! I'm enjoying Rome very much. I know lots of charming people here...' She talked like this for some time, then she turned to him and asked, 'Why didn't you come to visit me?' 6

'I've already told you,' Winterbourne replied. 'I've only just got off the train.'

'You must have stayed on the train a long time after it stopped!' said Daisy, with a little laugh. 'Anyway, you've had time to go and visit Mrs Walker.'

'I know Mrs Walker from Geneva —'

'I know. She told me. Well, you know me from Vevey. That's just as good. So you ought to have come to visit me.'

When they reached the Pincio, Daisy saw Mr Giovanelli. He was standing by a tree, looking at the women in their carriages. He was a handsome little man, very elegantly dressed, with a flower in his buttonhole.[1]

'Are you going to speak to that man?' asked Winterbourne.

'Of course!' said Daisy.

'Then I'm staying with you.'

Daisy stopped and looked at him for a moment in silence, but the expression on her face was still serene. 'I don't like the way you say that,' she said with a smile. 'I never allow gentlemen to tell me what to do.'

'I think you've made a mistake,' Winterbourne replied. 'You should sometimes listen to a gentleman — the right one.'

She looked at him again, more seriously this time, with her pretty eyes, then she laughed and said, 'I do nothing but listen to gentlemen! Is Mr Giovanelli the right one?'

Just then, Giovanelli saw them and walked up to them. He had a brilliant smile and intelligent eyes.

'No, he isn't the right one,' said Winterbourne.

Daisy introduced Giovanelli to Winterbourne, and they walked along, one gentleman on each side of Daisy. Mr Giovanelli spoke English very well. He made pleasant conversation with Winterbourne and Daisy. He was disappointed that Daisy had not come alone, but he did not show his disappointment. 'He's not a gentleman,' thought Winterbourne. 'He's a good imitation of

1. **buttonhole** : hole on the front of a jacket.

one, but a nice girl ought to know the difference!' But was Miss Daisy Miller a nice girl? That was the question. She had no delicacy, and yet she did not seem impatient for Winterbourne to go: she did not seem to want to be alone with her lover. She was a strange combination of audacity[1] and innocence.

Fifteen minutes later, Winterbourne noticed Mrs Walker sitting in her carriage at the side of the road. She waved to him. He left Miss Miller with Mr Giovanelli and went to Mrs Walker, who looked agitated. 'This is terrible!' said Mrs Walker. 'That girl mustn't do this kind of thing. She mustn't walk here with you two men. Fifty people have noticed her!'

'Is it really that important?' asked Winterbourne. 'She's very innocent.'

'She's very crazy!' cried Mrs Walker. 'And her mother is an absolute fool! When you left, I thought that, since her mother won't warn her,[2] I should, so I came here to find her. Tell her I want to speak to her.'

'I don't think it's a good idea,' said Winterbourne, 'but you can try.'

When Winterbourne gave Daisy this message, the young lady walked serenely to Mrs Walker's carriage with Mr Giovanelli at her side.

'Mrs Walker, this is Mr Giovanelli,' said Daisy prettily.

Mrs Walker nodded to the Italian then turned to Daisy and said, 'Will you get in the carriage and drive with me?'

'No, thank you,' said Daisy. 'I'm perfectly happy as I am.' And she smiled at her two gentlemen.

1. **audacity** : risky and courageous behaviour.
2. **warn her** : tell her of the possible danger of her actions.

'You may be perfectly happy, dear child, but it isn't the custom here[1] for a young lady to walk alone with gentlemen.'

'Well, it ought to be!' said Daisy. 'I love walking!'

'You should walk with your mother, dear,' said Mrs Walker.

'My mother never goes for a walk. And I'm not five years old!'

'You're old enough to be more reasonable,' said Mrs Walker. 'You're old enough, my dear Miss Miller, to cause a scandal.'

'What do you mean?' asked Daisy, smiling intensely.

'Come into my carriage, and I'll explain it to you,' Mrs Walker replied.

Daisy looked at Giovanelli then at Winterbourne. 'I don't think I want to know what you mean!' She blushed, and Winterbourne thought she was extremely pretty. She looked at Winterbourne and said, 'Do you think that – to save my reputation – I should get into the carriage?'

Winterbourne blushed a little and hesitated. It seemed so strange to hear her talk that way of her 'reputation'. He wanted to give the reply that was best for Daisy herself. He felt that it was in Daisy's best interest to hear the truth, and the truth, Winterbourne thought, was that she should do what Mrs Walker had asked her to do. He looked at her exquisite prettiness and then said, very gently, 'I think you should get into the carriage'.

Daisy gave a violent laugh. 'How ridiculous! If this is improper, Mrs Walker, then *I* am improper. Goodbye!' Then she turned and walked away with Mr Giovanelli.

Mrs Walker watched her go with tears in her eyes. 'Get in the carriage,' she said to Winterbourne.

1. **it isn't the custom here** : it is not usual or acceptable in this society.

'I think I should accompany Miss Miller.'

'If you don't get into this carriage, I'll never speak to you again!' cried Mrs Walker.

Winterbourne said goodbye to Daisy and Giovanelli and got into the carriage. 'That wasn't very clever of you,' he said.

'I'm not trying to be clever; I'm trying to be honest,' replied Mrs Walker. 'She's causing a great scandal. Italian men come to see her at her hotel late at night, when her mother has already gone to bed.'

'She's just unsophisticated,' said Winterbourne impatiently.

'She has no natural delicacy,' replied Mrs Walker. 'You must stop seeing her, stop flirting with her: leave her alone!'

'I can't do that. I like her very much.'

'Then you should want to protect her from scandal.'

Winterbourne got out of the carriage and said goodbye to Mrs Walker. He saw Daisy and Giovanelli standing by the wall, looking at the beautiful Villa Borghese. Giovanelli took Daisy's parasol and opened it. He rested the parasol on her shoulder so that both their heads were hidden behind it. Winterbourne hesitated a moment, then he turned and walked away, towards his aunt's house.

Go back to the text

1 Comprehension

Match the phrases in column A with the phrases in column B to form complete sentences.

A

1 ☐ Daisy was enjoying Rome
2 ☐ Daisy was angry with Winterbourne
3 ☐ Winterbourne told Daisy that he had not visited her earlier
4 ☐ Winterbourne was no longer certain that Daisy was a nice girl
5 ☐ Mrs Walker thought that Daisy was 'very crazy'
6 ☐ Mrs Walker thought she should tell Daisy not to walk alone with two men
7 ☐ Daisy did not get into the carriage with Mrs Walker
8 ☐ Winterbourne did not want to stop seeing Daisy

B

A because she did not realise that Mr Giovanelli was not a real gentleman.
B because he went to visit Mrs Walker first.
C because Daisy's mother had not warned her.
D because she knew many charming people there.
E because he liked her very much.
F because she liked walking and she did not care if she was improper.
G because she went walking alone with two men.
H because he had just got off the train.

2 Write about it

'Then *I* am improper'

Imagine you are Daisy's friend in America. Daisy wrote you a letter and described what happened with Mrs Walker at the Pincio. Write her a letter and say if you think she acted improperly or not.

You can begin your letter like this.

Dearest Daisy,
What an exciting time you are having in Rome! I was very interested to read about your experience with Mrs Walker. In my opinion ....
....
....
Your friend,
Adeline

FCE 3 The Pincio

Henry James fell in love with Italy, and, like Daisy, he adored the Pincio. Read this adaptation of Henry James's description of the Pincio from his book *Italian Hours*. Use the word given in capitals at the end of each line to form a word that fits in the space in the same line.

For the last few days I have spent a couple of hours in the sun of the Pincio.	
The weather was perfect, and the crowd,	
(1) .... today, was incredible.	PARTICULAR
Everybody was staring and friendly. All the	
(2) .... and half of the	NOBLE
(3) .... were there in their	FOREIGN
carriages, and the middle classes were on the ground staring at them.	
The great (4) .... between public	DIFFER
places in America and Europe is the number of people of every age and social status that stare at you, from your hat to your boots, as you pass.	
Europe is (5) .... the continent	CERTAIN

where people practise (6) .... The ladies at the Pincio have to walk past many people. In fact, (7) .... women learn how they must act in public when they are young.
A lady must travel in her carriage and ignore the men that stare at her on each side of the road. Then she must choose to notice and (8) .... greet just one of them.
This is one of her everyday jobs.
In any case, it is (9) .... to do nothing at all at the Pincio.

STARE
EUROPE
POLITE
WONDER

Before you read

1 In the next chapter, you will read about Mrs Walker's party. In pairs, discuss the following questions.

1 Considering their meeting at the Pincio, how do you think Mrs Miller will behave towards Daisy at the party?

2 What do you think Daisy's reaction will be?

2 Now look at the statements below. Listen to the beginning of Chapter Six and decide if they are true (T) or false (F). Correct the false ones.

		T	F
1	Mrs Miller came to the party with Eugenio.	☐	☐
2	Daisy came late to the party.	☐	☐
3	Mr Giovanelli did not come to the party.	☐	☐
4	Daisy refused to speak to Mrs Walker.	☐	☐
5	Mrs Walker was polite to Daisy.	☐	☐
6	Daisy sang songs all night.	☐	☐
7	Winterbourne ignored Daisy when she arrived.	☐	☐
8	Winterbourne did not want to dance.	☐	☐

CHAPTER **SIX**

Mrs Walker's Party

Mrs Walker's party was a few days later. Mrs Miller came alone. The poor lady was very nervous. 'I've never been to a party alone before, especially in this country!' she told Mrs Walker, 'I wanted to bring Randolph or Eugenio, but Daisy told me to go alone!'

'Is your daughter going to favour us with her company?' asked Mrs Walker, but Mrs Miller did not notice her sarcasm.

'Well, she's dressed for the party. She got dressed before dinner. But her friend is there – the Italian gentleman. Daisy's playing the piano and Mr Giovanelli's singing. He sings splendidly. But I think they'll come soon,' said Mrs Miller hopefully.

Mrs Walker turned to Winterbourne and said, 'This is horrible! Miss Miller is trying to punish me for criticising her in the Pincio the other day. When she comes, I won't speak to her!'

Daisy came after eleven o'clock. 'I'm sorry I'm late,' she said to Mrs Walker with a smile. 'Mr Giovanelli and I were practising his songs so that he can sing for your guests. He has such a beautiful voice.' Daisy looked very lovely as she said this in her sweet, bright voice. 'Is there anyone here I know?' she asked, looking around with interest at the other guests.

'I think everyone knows who you are!' said Mrs Walker coldly.

Mr Giovanelli sang his songs very well, although no one had asked him to do so. Daisy talked as he sang. 'I'd love to dance,' she said to Winterbourne, 'but these rooms are too small.'

'I don't want to dance,' Winterbourne replied. 'I can't dance.' END

'Of course you can't dance; you're too stiff.' [1] said Miss Daisy. 'I hope you enjoyed your ride in Mrs Walker's carriage.'

'No, I didn't enjoy it. I preferred walking with you.'

'You went with your friend, and I went with mine. That was much better. But really, Mrs Walker has such strange ideas!' continued Daisy. 'How could I get into her carriage and leave poor Mr Giovanelli?'

'Mr Giovanelli was wrong to ask you to walk with him. No young Italian lady walks with gentlemen in the streets.'

'In the streets?' cried Daisy. 'The Pincio is not "the streets"! And fortunately I'm not a young Italian lady! It seems to me they have a miserable time!'

'People here think you're a flirt,' said Winterbourne seriously.

'Of course I am!' said Daisy with a smile. 'All nice girls are flirts! But I suppose you'll say that I'm not a nice girl.'

'You're a very nice girl,' said Winterbourne, 'but I want you to flirt with me and nobody else.'

'Thank you!' replied Daisy. 'But I don't want to flirt with you: you're too stiff!'

1. **stiff** : rigid; (here) formal and conventional.

'Well, at least stop flirting with Giovanelli. They don't understand that sort of thing here.'

'I thought they understood nothing else!' said Daisy.

'Not in young unmarried women.'

'It seems to me much more proper in young unmarried women than in old married ones,' cried Daisy.

'Well,' said Winterbourne, 'you must obey the customs of the place. Flirting is a purely American custom; it doesn't exist here. So when you go out in public with Mr Giovanelli and without your mother, people are shocked.'

'Poor Mother!' said Daisy.

'You are flirting, but Mr Giovanelli isn't: he's quite serious.'

'At least he doesn't tell me what to do!' cried Daisy. 'Anyway, I'm not flirting with Mr Giovanelli. We're good friends, very intimate friends.'

'Ah,' replied Winterbourne, 'it's different if you're in love with each other.'

To Winterbourne's surprise, Daisy blushed and stood up angrily. 'At least Mr Giovanelli never says such horrible things!' she cried.

Daisy spent the rest of the evening sitting with Mr Giovanelli in a quiet corner of the room. When she came back to say goodbye to Mrs Walker, the lady ignored her. Daisy went pale and looked anxiously at her mother. Winterbourne felt very sorry for her.

'That was very cruel,' he said to Mrs Walker, after Daisy had left.

'I'll never invite her here again!' Mrs Walker replied.

In the weeks that followed, Winterbourne often went to visit Daisy at her hotel. Giovanelli was always there, but Daisy did not

seem disturbed by Winterbourne's presence. It seemed that she could talk as happily with one gentleman or two.

One Sunday afternoon, Winterbourne went to St Peter's with his aunt. When he saw Daisy and Giovanelli walking together in the great church, he said to his aunt, 'There's Miss Miller!'

Mrs Costello looked at Daisy for a moment then said, 'Is that what makes you so distracted these days?'

'I'm not distracted,' replied Winterbourne.

'You seem very preoccupied: you're thinking of something.'

'And what do you think I'm thinking of?'

'Of Miss Miller's intimacy with that ridiculous Italian,' said Mrs Costello, indicating Giovanelli.

'I don't think it's an "intimacy" in the sense you mean.'

'Everyone else does. He's very handsome, and she's very vulgar. She thinks he's the most elegant gentleman in the world. He's even better than the courier! The courier probably introduced them, and when they're married this man will give the courier a lot of money. Yes, I see how it is.'

'I don't believe she's thinking of marrying him,' said Winterbourne, 'and I don't think he hopes to marry her.'

'She's so vulgar that she probably doesn't think at all,' said Mrs Costello. 'But believe me, very soon she'll tell you that she's engaged.'

'I don't think so,' Winterbourne replied. 'I've asked some questions about him. He's a perfectly respectable little man, but he's not from the best Italian society. He has no money and no title — he's not a count or a marchese [1] — so he knows that he cannot hope to marry her. He probably doesn't realise that Daisy

1. **count or a marchese** : two aristocratic titles.

and her mother aren't sophisticated enough to want to catch a count or a marchese.'

'He thinks he can win her with his handsome face,' said Mrs Costello.

'No,' replied Winterbourne. 'He knows that he has nothing but his handsome face, and he knows that Mr Miller, in the

mysterious land of dollars, will want his daughter to marry someone with more than that.'

Some of Mrs Costello's American friends joined them then, and Winterbourne heard a lot of talk about the scandalous Miss Daisy Miller. He felt sorry for her. He was sorry to hear them talking about her like that: to him she seemed just pretty and unprotected and natural.

Go back to the text

FCE 1 Comprehension

For questions 1-5, choose the answer (A, B, C or D) which you think fits best according to the text.

1 Mrs Walker tells Daisy that everyone knows who she is. She means that

A ☐ Daisy is so pretty that everyone notices her.
B ☐ her scandalous actions have made her known to everybody.
C ☐ there are few American girls in Rome and so everybody knows her.
D ☐ she is Winterbourne's friend and so everybody knows her.

2 Daisy believes that all nice girls

A ☐ are miserable.
B ☐ do not flirt with someone as stiff as Winterbourne.
C ☐ are flirts.
D ☐ only flirt with one gentleman.

3 Winterbourne is not angry that Daisy flirts but

A ☐ he does not want her to do it in public.
B ☐ he wants her to flirt only with him.
C ☐ he does not want Mrs Walker to know about it.
D ☐ he does not want his aunt to know about it.

4 Daisy became angry with Winterbourne because he said that

A ☐ she flirted with every gentleman she met.
B ☐ she should only flirt with him.
C ☐ she was in love with Mr Giovanelli.
D ☐ Mr Giovanelli was not really in love with her.

5 How was Mrs Walker cruel to Daisy at the party?

A ☐ She decided not to invite her to any more parties.
B ☐ She did not say goodbye to her at the end of the party.
C ☐ She did not listen to Mr Giovanelli sing.
D ☐ She said that Daisy and Mr Giovanelli were lovers.

T: GRADE 7

2 **Topic — National customs**

Frederick tells Daisy, 'You must obey the customs of the place. Flirting is a purely American custom; it doesn't exist here.' Choose one or two distinctive customs of your country and prepare to talk about them. Use the following questions to help you.

- Does everybody in your country follow this/these customs?
- Where do these customs come from?
- What should a person from another country know about these customs?

3 **Summing it up**

Number the following paragraphs in the right order to make a summary of Chapters 4-6. Then fill in the gaps with the words in the box.

alone	criticised	fortune-hunters	innocent	agreed	
handsome	practising	friend	goodbye	improper	meet

A ☐ Daisy announced that she was going to .... Mr Giovanelli at the Pincio. Mrs Walker said she should not go alone so Winterbourne .... to accompany her.

B ☐ Daisy disagreed with her and walked away with Mr Giovanelli. A few days later, Mrs Miller arrived .... at Mrs Walker's party. She said that Daisy was at home .... some songs with Mr Giovanelli.

C ☐ When Winterbourne arrived in Rome in January, he went to see his aunt. She told him that Daisy was often seen with young Roman ...., and one very .... one in particular. He was hurt and so he decided to go and see his friend Mrs Walker first.

D ☐ When they arrived, they saw the young Italian. Then after fifteen minutes Mrs Walker arrived in a carriage. She tried to convince Daisy that it was .... to walk with two gentlemen.

E ☐ Mrs Walker was certain that Daisy did this to offend her because she had .... her at the Pincio. So, at the end of the evening, Mrs Walker did not even say .... to Daisy.

F ☐ When he was at Mrs Walker's house, Daisy and her family arrived. Daisy then asked Mrs Walker if she could bring a .... to Mrs Walker's party. This friend was an Italian called Mr Giovanelli.

G ☐ In the weeks that followed Winterbourne visited Daisy at her hotel. He still believed she was .... and was sad to hear people talk badly about her.

Before you read

8 FCE

1 Listening

Listen to the beginning of Chapter Seven. For questions 1-6, complete the sentences with a word or phrase.

1 When Winterbourne went to see Daisy at the hotel, Daisy was ....

2 Mrs Miller thinks that Mr Giovanelli is a real ....

3 Mrs Miller thinks that Daisy .... as if she was engaged.

4 Mrs Miller wants Mr Giovanelli to tell her if they become engaged because she wants to ....

5 The American residents in Rome wanted their Italian friends to know that Daisy was not ....

6 Winterbourne could not decide whether Daisy was a rebellious young woman or ....

CHAPTER **SEVEN**

Innocent or Immoral?

A few days later, Winterbourne went to see Mrs Miller at her hotel, hoping to persuade her to take better care of her daughter. 8

'I'm sorry, Daisy isn't here,' said Mrs Miller. 'She's gone somewhere with Mr Giovanelli. She's always going somewhere with Mr Giovanelli.'

'I've noticed that they're very intimate,' said Winterbourne.

'Oh! It seems as if they couldn't live without each other!' said Mrs Miller. 'Well, at least he's a real gentleman. I keep telling Daisy that she's engaged!'

'And what does Daisy say?'

'Oh, she says she isn't engaged, but she acts as if she is! I asked Mr Giovanelli to tell me if they get engaged, so that I can write and tell Mr Miller.'

Winterbourne had never heard a parent speak of a daughter's behaviour in such a distant way. He found Mrs Miller's attitude so strange and confusing that he gave up the idea of warning her.

After that, Winterbourne noticed that Daisy was no longer invited to people's houses. Society had decided that Miss Daisy Miller had gone too far. [1] How did she feel about that? Sometimes he thought she did not care: she was too childish and superficial to notice what people thought of her. At other moments he thought she knew perfectly well the impression she produced, but she refused to change because she knew that she was innocent. But then he thought perhaps she refused to change because she was irresponsible. It was becoming more and more difficult for him to believe in her innocence.

He was angry with himself because he could not decide what kind of young lady Miss Daisy Miller was. He had no idea whether her eccentricities [2] were personal or national. By not inviting her to their parties, the other American residents in Rome were sending a clear message to their Italian friends, who were all aristocrats. They were telling the Italians that, though Miss Daisy Miller was an American young lady, she was not typical. So perhaps Daisy's eccentricities were purely personal. But was she innocent or immoral? Did she understand the consequences of her actions, or was she ignorant of them? Was she simply a child, or was she a rebellious young woman? END

One day, he met her in the Palace of the Caesars. She was walking through the flowers in the beautiful deserted gardens with Mr Giovanelli.

1. **Miss Daisy Miller had gone too far** : (here) her behaviour was too scandalous and unacceptable.
2. **eccentricities** : strange, unusual ways of behaving and thinking.

'Aren't you lonely?' asked Daisy.

'Lonely?'

'Yes. You're always walking around alone. Can't you find anyone to walk with you?'

'I'm not as fortunate as your companion,' replied Winterbourne.

From the first, Giovanelli had treated Winterbourne with great courtesy and respect. He had listened to Winterbourne's conversation and laughed whenever Winterbourne said something amusing. He gave the impression that he considered Winterbourne a superior young man. He did not act like a jealous lover. Obviously, Giovanelli was very diplomatic. He did not mind showing a little humility in front of the American. At times, it even seemed to Winterbourne that Giovanelli wanted to talk to him privately – to explain that of course he, Giovanelli, knew that this young lady was too good for him. On this occasion, he walked away from his companions and went to pick some flowers for his buttonhole.

'I know why you say that,' said Daisy. 'You think I spend too much time with Mr Giovanelli.'

'Everyone thinks so.'

'They don't really care what I do,' Daisy replied.

'Oh yes, they do, and they'll be very unpleasant to you. They're already being unpleasant to you. Haven't you noticed?'

'I've noticed you,' said Daisy. 'But I noticed that you were very stiff and conventional the first time I saw you!'

'I'm not as stiff as some of the others,' said Winterbourne, smiling. 'Haven't you noticed that they don't invite you to their houses anymore?'

'Why do you let people be so unkind?' cried Daisy.

'What can I do?' replied Winterbourne.

'You could say something to them.'

'I do say something. I say that your mother thinks you're engaged.'

'Well, she does,' said Daisy very simply.

'And does Randolph believe it?' asked Winterbourne, laughing.

'I don't know. I don't think he believes anything,' she replied, 'and since you've mentioned it, I *am* engaged.'

Winterbourne stopped laughing and looked at her in surprise.

'You don't believe it!' cried Daisy.

He was silent a moment and then said, 'Yes, I believe it.'

'Oh no, you don't!' she replied. 'Well, then – I'm not!'

Go back to the text

1 Comprehension

Answer the following questions.

1 Why did Winterbourne go to see Mrs Miller?
2 What did Winterbourne find confusing about Mrs Miller?
3 How did Roman society react to Daisy's behaviour?
4 Why was Winterbourne angry with himself?
5 According to Winterbourne, what did Giovanelli himself think of his relationship with Daisy?
6 How did Winterbourne defend Daisy against her critics?
7 At first, what did Daisy tell Winterbourne about being engaged to Giovanelli? In the end what did she say?

2 Vocabulary

Find a word from the text of Chapter Seven that means the same as the definitions below (1-7). To help you, some of the letters have already been given.

1 A person's way of acting: _ _ h _ _ _ _ u _
2 Not thinking carefully about the results of your actions: _ _ _ _ _ p _ _ _ _ b _ _
3 Going against conventional, accepted ideas; opposing authority: r _ _ _ l l _ _ _ _
4 Empty, with no one there: _ _ _ _ _ _ e _
5 Politeness, respect and consideration for others: _ _ u _ _ _ _ y
6 Able to do and say things in a careful way that does not cause offence: _ _ _ l _ _ _ _ i _
7 Unkind, not very nice: _ n _ _ _ _ _ _ n _

3 Daisy's eccentricities

Discuss these questions with your partner. Then present your conclusions to the class.

1 Do you think Winterbourne would worry about Daisy's eccentricities if Daisy decided to flirt only with him?

2 Daisy thinks that the Americans don't really care what she does. She also says — in the original novel — that they just pretend to be shocked by her actions. Do you agree with her?

3 Do you think Daisy has the right attitude towards society life in Rome?

'I asked Mr Giovanelli to tell me if they get engaged'

Look at how we report the following orders and requests:

'Can you help me carry this bag?' said Daisy to Eugenio.
→ *Daisy asked Eugenio to help her carry the bag.*

'Randolph, go to bed!' shouted Daisy.
→ *Daisy ordered Randolph to go to bed.*

'Don't touch that sculpture, Randolph!' shouted Mrs Miller.
→ *Mrs Miller told Randolph not to touch the sculpture.*

4 Change the following commands into reported speech.

1 'Don't drink the local water,' the doctor said to Mrs Miller.

....

2 'Stop running, Randolph,' said Mrs Miller.

....

3 'Don't spend time with that horrible Daisy Miller,' Mrs Costello told Frederick.

....

5 Change the following reported requests into direct speech.

1 Winterbourne asked the driver to take him to the Pincio.

....

2 Daisy asked the waiter to bring her a glass of lemonade.

....

3 Randolph asked Daisy to give him some candy.

....

▶▶▶ INTERNET PROJECT ◀◀◀

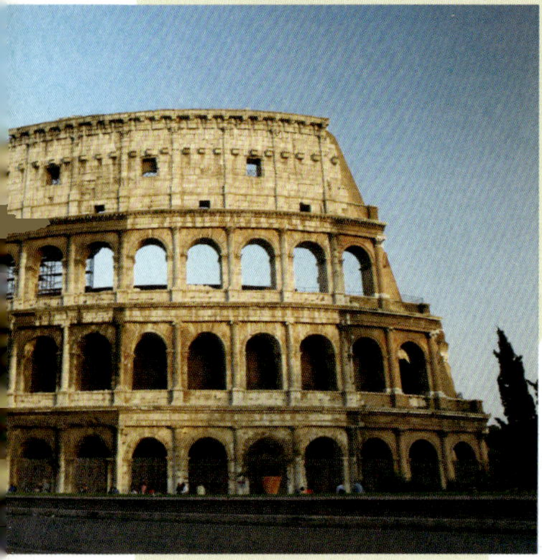

The Colosseum

I stood within the Colosseum's wall
Midst the chief relics of Almighty Rome –
The trees which grew along the
* broken arches*
Waved dark in the blue midnight
* Manfred (1877) by Lord Byron*

Connect to the Internet and go to www.blackcat-cideb.com or www.cideb.it. Insert the title or part of the title of the book into our search engine. Open the page for *Daisy Miller*. Click on the Internet project link. Go down the page until you find the title of this book and click on the relevant link for this project. Answer the following questions about the Colosseum.

1 When was it built?

2 How did it get its name?

3 In Roman times the following events were held in the Colosseum:

Naumachiae Venationes Silvae Munera

What were these events? Download some pictures you like and explain them to your class.

Before you read

1 Listen to the beginning of Chapter Eight and decide if the following statements are true (T) or false (F).

		T	F
1	Winterbourne was walking home with friends.	☐	☐
2	Both poets and doctors had the same view of the Colosseum.	☐	☐
3	Winterbourne did not want to stay for very long.	☐	☐
4	He saw two people sitting on the base of the cross.	☐	☐
5	He recognised Daisy by her voice.	☐	☐

CHAPTER **EIGHT**

A Night at the Colosseum

A week later, Winterbourne was walking home alone at eleven o'clock at night after dinner with friends. He decided to go into the Colosseum. Outside, he noticed a carriage was waiting. He walked into the silent arena in the moonlight. One half of the gigantic circus was in shadow. The place had never seemed more splendid, and he remembered Byron's famous lines. [1] But then he thought, 'The poets love the Colosseum by night, but the doctors say it's dangerous because of the risk of getting malaria. I should go soon.'

1. **Byron's famous lines** : the dramatic poem *Manfred* (1817) by the great English poet Byron (1788-1824) describes the Colosseum seen by moonlight.

As he walked towards the great cross [1] in the centre of the arena, he saw that two people were on the steps at its base. One, a woman, was sitting on a step; her companion was standing beside her. Then Winterbourne heard the woman's voice: 'He looks at us as one of those old lions must have looked at the Christians!' It was the voice of Miss Daisy Miller.

'Let's hope he's not very hungry,' Giovanelli replied with a laugh.

Winterbourne stopped. He felt a combination of horror and relief. [2] Now at last he knew what to think of Miss Daisy Miller: she was not a respectable young lady. He felt angry with himself for having spent so much time trying to decide what to think of her. He turned to walk out of the Colosseum, but then she spoke again: 'It's Mr Winterbourne! He saw me, and he didn't say hello!'

How cleverly she played the part of the innocent! But he could not just ignore her. As he walked towards the great cross, Daisy stood up and Giovanelli raised his hat. Winterbourne now began to think how crazy she was to be there. A delicate young girl should not spend the evening in the Colosseum: she might get Roman fever. 'It's now clear,' thought Winterbourne, 'that she's an immoral young woman, but even so I don't want her to die of malaria.'

'How long have you been here?' he asked angrily.

Daisy, lovely in the moonlight, looked at him for a moment then said gently, 'We've been here all evening. Isn't it pretty?'

'You could get malaria! You won't think that's pretty!' cried Winterbourne. Then, turning to Giovanelli, he's said, 'You're a

1. **the great cross** : a monument to the Christians who were killed in the Colosseum. It is no longer there.
2. **relief** : a feeling of happiness after something unpleasant has ended.

Roman. You know about Roman fever. Why did you bring her here?'

'Ah,' said the handsome Roman, 'I'm not afraid of getting malaria myself.'

'But what about this young lady?'

'I told the Signorina that it was dangerous, but she's never cautious.'

'I've never been ill a day in my life!' said Daisy. 'I wanted to see the Colosseum by moonlight, and we've had a lovely time. When I get home, Eugenio will give me some of his medicine against malaria. He has some splendid pills.'

'Well, go home now and take one!' cried Winterbourne.

Giovanelli went out to find the carriage. Daisy followed with Winterbourne. She did not seem at all embarrassed. She talked about the beauty of the place and how glad she was to have seen it by moonlight. Then she noticed that Winterbourne was silent.

'Why are you so quiet?' she asked.

Winterbourne did not reply but began to laugh.

'Did you believe that I was engaged the other day?' she asked.

'It doesn't matter what I believed the other day,' replied Winterbourne, still laughing. 'Now I believe it makes very little difference whether you're engaged or not!'

Daisy looked at him, but in the darkness he could not see her face. Then Giovanelli came to say that the carriage was ready.

'Don't forget to take Eugenio's pills!' said Winterbourne.

Daisy replied in a trembling voice, 'I don't care whether I get Roman fever or not!' Then she got into the carriage, and it drove off.

Go back to the text

1 Comprehension

Match the phrases in column A with the phrases in column B to form complete sentences.

A

1 ☐ The Colosseum seemed especially splendid that night
2 ☐ Winterbourne decided to leave the Colosseum
3 ☐ Winterbourne finally decided that Daisy was not a nice girl
4 ☐ Winterbourne felt angry with himself
5 ☐ Winterbourne thought that Daisy was crazy
6 ☐ Daisy went to the Colosseum
7 ☐ Daisy was not afraid of getting malaria
8 ☐ Giovanelli left Daisy and Winterbourne alone

B

A because he had spent so much time trying to form an opinion of Daisy.
B because Eugenio had pills against it.
C because he saw her alone with Giovanelli in the Colosseum.
D because the moon shone on it.
E because she could get malaria at night in the Colosseum.
F because he thought he could get malaria.
G because he went to look for their carriage.
H because she wanted to see it by moonlight.

FCE 2 Roman fever

Read the text on malaria below and think of the word that best fits each space. Use only one word in each space. There are two examples at the beginning (0 and 00).

The Roman fever mentioned (**0**) ....in.......... *Daisy Miller* is actually malaria. Malaria is (**00**) ....an.......... Italian word that (**1**) .... 'bad air'. In fact, the real cause of malaria — microorganisms — (**2**) .... not known until 1880. Before this, people (**3**) .... that you got the disease from humid night air.

Malaria still kills around two million people a year in tropical countries. But in temperate countries it (**4**) .... been mostly eliminated: this happened in North America in the 1880s and in Italy in the 1950s. It is interesting to note that the cure (**5**) .... malaria is directly connected with Rome. In 1623, ten cardinals died of malaria while electing the new pope. When the new pope, Urban VIII, was elected he instructed his missionaries to (**6**) .... for a cure. It was a Jesuit missionary in Peru who found the cure: quinine. Quinine comes (**7**) .... the bark (the outside layer) of a tree — the ancient Incas used it to fight fevers. This became one of the first modern drugs used to fight a disease, and by 1880 (**8**) .... were even pills of quinine in Rome that tourists like Daisy Miller could take. The British in India also took quinine. They found a way to make this bitter substance (**9**) .... pleasant by mixing it with soda water and lime. (**10**) .... is the origin of the famous Schweppes tonic water.

Before you read

1 Read the beginning of Chapter Nine below. For questions 1-6, choose the word you think is correct.

Winterbourne (**1**) said/told no one that he had met Miss Miller at eleven o'clock in the Colosseum with a gentleman. Nevertheless, two days later, all the American residents in Rome knew about it and were (**2**) talking/saying about 'the little American flirt'. Winterbourne found that he no (**3**) more/longer cared that people were saying unkind things about Daisy Miller.

Then he heard that Daisy was (**4**) much/very ill. He went to the hotel to ask how she was. There he met three other visitors who said that Daisy was dangerously ill: she had a (**5**) terribly/terrible case of malaria. He did not see Mrs Miller: finally that lady was where she (**6**) should/must always have been — at her daughter's side.

10 **Now listen to the recording to check your answers.**

CHAPTER **NINE**

Daisy Becomes Ill

Winterbourne told no one that he had met Miss Miller at eleven o'clock in the Colosseum with a gentleman. Nevertheless, two days later, all the American residents in Rome knew about it and were talking about 'the little American flirt'. Winterbourne found that he no longer cared that people were saying unkind things about Daisy Miller. 10

Then he heard that Daisy was very ill. He went to the hotel to ask how she was. There he met three other visitors who said that Daisy was dangerously ill: she had a terrible case of malaria. He did not see Mrs Miller: finally that lady was where she should always have been — at her daughter's side. END

Winterbourne went to the hotel often to ask for news of Daisy. One time he saw Mrs Miller. 'Daisy spoke of you the other day,' said Daisy's mother. 'Half the time she's delirious from the fever and she doesn't know what she's saying, but that time I think she did. She told me to tell you that she was never engaged to that handsome Italian. I was very glad to hear that: Mr Giovanelli hasn't been to see us since she got ill. A lady told me that he's afraid that I'm angry with him for taking Daisy out at night. Well, I am angry with him, but I'm a lady: even when I'm angry I can be polite to guests. Anyway, Daisy said she's not engaged. I don't know why she wanted you to know. She told me three times. "Be sure to tell Mr Winterbourne" she said. And then she told me to ask if you remember the time you went to that castle in Switzerland.'

A week later, the poor girl died. Daisy's grave [1] was in the little Protestant cemetery by the wall of imperial Rome, beneath the cypress trees and the spring flowers. Winterbourne was surprised by the number of people present at the funeral. Many people who had been unkind to her when she was alive came to pay their last respects [2] now that she was dead. Giovanelli stood near Winterbourne. He was very pale. On this occasion he had no flower in his buttonhole.

When the funeral was over, Giovanelli turned to Winterbourne and said, 'She was the most beautiful young lady I ever saw, and the nicest.' He was silent for a moment, then he said, 'And she was the most innocent.'

Winterbourne looked at him then repeated his words, 'And the most innocent?'

1. **grave** : a place where someone is buried.
2. **pay their last respects** : to honour someone after their death by attending their funeral.

'The most innocent!'

Winterbourne felt very angry. 'Why the devil,' he asked, 'did you take her to that fatal place?'

Mr Giovanelli was silent for a moment, then he said, 'I had no fear for myself, and she wanted to go.'

'That's no reason!' cried Winterbourne.

Giovanelli was silent again, and then he said, 'She didn't want to marry me. For a while I hoped, but now I'm sure that she didn't want to.'

Winterbourne listened to him. He looked down at the new grave surrounded by April flowers. When he looked up again, Mr Giovanelli had gone.

Winterbourne left Rome soon afterwards. In the months that followed, he often thought about Daisy Miller and her mysterious manners. The following summer, he went to see his aunt Mrs Costello in Vevey. One day he spoke to her about Daisy.

'I think I treated her unfairly,' he said. 'She sent me a message before her death which I didn't understand at the time. But I have thought about it since, and now I understand. She wanted me to respect her.'

'Is that a modest way of saying she wanted you to love her?' asked Mrs Costello.

Winterbourne did not reply to this question. After a short silence, he continued: 'What you said last summer was true: I did make a great mistake. I've lived too long in foreign countries.'

Nevertheless, he went back to Geneva. His friends say that he is 'studying' there. Other people say that he is interested in a very clever foreign lady.

Go back to the text

1 Comprehension

Say whether the following statements are true (T) or false (F), and then correct the false ones.

		T	F
1	All the Americans in Rome knew that Daisy had been at the Colosseum.	☐	☐
2	Daisy became ill with Roman fever.	☐	☐
3	Daisy was delirious when she said that she was not really engaged to Giovanelli.	☐	☐
4	Mrs Miller was angry with Mr Giovanelli.	☐	☐
5	Daisy had wanted to know if Winterbourne remembered their hotel in Switzerland.	☐	☐
6	Only the people who really liked Daisy came to her funeral.	☐	☐
7	Giovanelli did not think that Daisy was an innocent girl.	☐	☐
8	Winterbourne still didn't understand Daisy's final message to him.	☐	☐

FCE 2 The final verdict

Imagine you are Frederick Winterbourne. Write a letter to a friend and explain what you now think about Daisy Miller. You should write between 120-180 words.

In your letter explain:

- *The different opinions you have had of Daisy*
- *What you thought when you saw her in the Colosseum*
- *Why you think she wanted you to know that she was not engaged*
- *Your final opinion of her*

Dear Henry,

Do you remember me talking about Miss Daisy Miller? Well, ...

Your friend,

Frederick

FCE 3 The Protestant cemetery of Rome

For questions 1-18, read the text below and look carefully at each line. Some of the lines are correct, and some have a word which should not be there. If a line is correct, put a tick (✓). If a line has a word which should not be there, write the word.There are two examples at the beginning (0 and 00).

0 The fictional Daisy Miller was buried in the real
00 Protestant cemetery of Rome. It is located there behind
1 the Pyramid of Cestius, which was built in the 30 BC.
2 Its Italian name, *Cimitero acattolico*,
3 or 'non-Catholic cemetery', is it more precise.
4 It was founded in the 1700s because
5 non-Catholics could not be buried
6 in the city of the Rome, and at that time
7 the Protestant cemetery was in the countryside
8 just outside of Rome. This cemetery that contains the tombs
9 of two of England's most greatest poets,
10 John Keats (1795-1821) and Percy Bysshe Shelley (1792-1822).
11 John Keats died from tuberculosis. However,
12 his friends thought how he died because
13 his poetry was been cruelly criticised. In fact,
14 the inscription on his tomb speaks of his 'malicious enemies'.
15 Keats himself wrote that he was a person
16 whose name was 'written on water'.
17 One thing is certain, both the Keats and Shelley would
18 have understood about the poetic death of Daisy Miller.

0 ...✓...... 00 ...there... 1 .... 2 .... 3 .... 4 ....
5 .... 6 .... 7 .... 8 .... 9 .... 10 ....
11 .... 12 .... 13 .... 14 .... 15 .... 16 ....
17 .... 18 ....

4 Summing it up

Read the summary of Chapters Seven to Nine. Five sentences have been removed from the text. Choose from the sentences A-E the one which fits each gap (1-5).

Winterbourne went to see Mrs Miller. He wanted to tell her to take better care of her daughter.

1 ....

He told her that people were talking unkindly about her. Winterbourne said that he defended her by saying her mother thought she was engaged.

2 ....

A week later Winterbourne was walking by the Colosseum at night. He saw Daisy and Giovanelli alone inside. Now he was certain that Daisy was not a 'nice girl'.

3 ....

Soon after that evening, Daisy became very ill with malaria. Winterbourne went to see her at her hotel.

4 ....

A week later Daisy died. Many people who had been unkind to her came to her funeral. Giovanelli was there too.

5 ....

Winterbourne realised that he had not really understood Daisy at all.

A He went up to them. He told Daisy that she should go to the hotel immediately. It was very dangerous to be outside at night.

B He did not see Daisy, but Mrs Miller gave him a message from Daisy: she wanted him to know that she was never really engaged.

C He told Winterbourne that Daisy was the most innocent young lady he ever met.

D Daisy then said she really was engaged. When Winterbourne appeared upset by this news, Daisy told him that she wasn't.

E But Mrs Miller did not seem worried about Daisy. Then Winterbourne met Daisy with Giovanelli in the Palace of the Caesars.

FCE **1** **Choose the correct answer A, B, C or D.**

1 Where did Frederick go to school and university?
A ☐ Paris
B ☐ New York
C ☐ Vevey
D ☐ Geneva

2 The first time Frederick talked with Daisy he felt embarrassed because
A ☐ they had not been formally introduced.
B ☐ she was very attractive.
C ☐ he could not understand if she was flirting.
D ☐ he had given her brother sugar without permission.

3 How did Daisy discover that Frederick's aunt did not want to meet her?
A ☐ Frederick told her.
B ☐ She understood by herself.
C ☐ Eugenio told her.
D ☐ Mrs Miller told her.

4 How did Frederick consider his trip to the castle with Daisy?
A ☐ as a formal obligation
B ☐ as an enjoyable excursion
C ☐ as a romantic adventure
D ☐ as a chance to escape his aunt

5 How had Frederick imagined Daisy before his arrival in Rome?
A ☐ Talking and dancing with elegant Italian gentlemen.
B ☐ In her hotel room waiting for him to arrive.
C ☐ Walking around Rome with her mother, brother and courier.
D ☐ Enjoying herself in the houses of respectable Americans.

6 Daisy was happy in Rome because
A ☐ she loved visiting the historic sites.
B ☐ she was meeting a lot of nice gentlemen.
C ☐ Frederick came to see her there.
D ☐ the hotel rooms were so beautiful.

7 Mrs Miller did not think Daisy should go to the Pincio because

A ☐ she was worried about her becoming ill.
B ☐ she thought it was improper.
C ☐ she did not like Mr Giovanelli.
D ☐ she did not want to be left alone.

8 At the party, how did Mrs Walker show Daisy that she was offended?

A ☐ She did not let Mr Giovanelli sing.
B ☐ She did not compliment her on her pretty dress.
C ☐ She did not say goodbye to her when she left.
D ☐ She did not say hello to Mr Giovanelli.

9 Winterbourne discovered that Mr Giovanelli was really

A ☐ a courier.
B ☐ a count.
C ☐ a marchese.
D ☐ a man with no title.

10 How did Frederick defend Daisy when people spoke badly about her?

A ☐ He said that she was a nice girl.
B ☐ He said that all American girls flirt.
C ☐ He said that Mrs Miller thought she was engaged.
D ☐ He said that she and Mr Giovanelli were just good friends.

11 When Frederick saw Daisy in the Colosseum he decided that she was

A ☐ not a respectable young lady.
B ☐ a flirt.
C ☐ engaged to Mr Giovanelli.
D ☐ not engaged to Mr Giovanelli.

12 When Daisy was ill she told her mother to tell Frederick that

A ☐ she really was engaged to Mr Giovanelli.
B ☐ she really loved him and not Mr Giovanelli.
C ☐ she was never engaged to Mr Giovanelli.
D ☐ he must not be so stiff.

Key to Exit Test

1 1D 2A 3B 4C 5B 6B 7B 8C 9D 10C 11A 12C

The new structures introduced in this step of our READING & TRAINING series are listed below. Any one reader may not always include all of the structures listed, but it will certainly not include any structures from higher steps. Naturally, structures from lower steps will be included. For a complete list of all the structures used over all the six steps, consult the *Black Cat Guide to Graded Readers*, which is also available online at our website, www.blackcat-cideb.com or www.cideb.it.

Apart from the structural control, we also take great care to grade the vocabulary appropriately for each step.

Step Four B2.1

All the structures used in the previous levels, plus the following:

Verb tenses
Present Perfect Simple: *the first / second* etc. *time that ...*
Present Perfect Continuous: unfinished past with *for* or *since* (duration form)

Verb forms and patterns
Passive forms: Present Perfect Simple
Reported speech introduced by precise reporting verbs (e.g. *suggest*, *promise*, *apologise*)

Modal verbs
Be / get used to + *-ing*: habit formation
Had better: duty and warning

Types of clause
3rd Conditional: *if* + Past Perfect, *would(n't) have*
Conditionals with *may / might*
Non-defining relative clauses with: *which*, *whose*
Clauses of concession: *even though*; *in spite of*, *despite*

Also available at Step Four:

- **American Horror** Edgar Allan Poe
- **Beowulf**
- **The Big Mistake and Other Stories** Nella Burnett-Stuart and Bruna Deriu
- **The Canterbury Tales** Geoffrey Chaucer
- **A Christmas Carol** Charles Dickens
- **Daisy Miller** Henry James
- **Dracula** Bram Stoker
- **Famous British Criminals from The Newgate Calendar**
- **Jack the Ripper** Peter Foreman
- **The Last of the Mohicans** James Fenimore Cooper
- **Macbeth** William Shakespeare
- **The Merchant of Venice** William Shakespeare
- **A Midsummer Night's Dream** William Shakespeare
- **Le Morte d'Arthur** Sir Thomas Malory
- **Much Ado About Nothing** William Shakespeare
- **Othello** William Shakespeare
- **The Secret Agent** Joseph Conrad
- **A Study in Scarlet** Sir Arthur Conan Doyle
- **Tom Jones** Henry Fielding
- **The Tragedy of Dr Faustus** Christopher Marlowe
- **The Turn of the Screw** Henry James
- **Washington Square** Henry James
- **Wicked and Humorous Tales** Saki